Making Jesus My Best Friend

Baptism Preparation for Younger Children
(ages 8-10)

Claudio and Pamela Consuegra

REVIEW AND HERALD® PUBLISHING ASSOCIATION
Since 1861 | www.reviewandherald.com

To order additional copies of *Making Jesus My Best Friend*,
by Claudio and Pamela Consuegra, **call 1-800-765-6955.**

Visit us at www.reviewandherald.com for information
on other Review and Herald® products.

This book was
Edited by Patricia Fritz
Copyedited by James Cavil
Cover design by Freshcut
Cover art from Goodsalt.com / Lars Justinen
Interior design by Candy Harvey
Electronic makeup by Shirley M. Bolivar
Typeset: 12/16 Cheltenham

PRINTED IN U.S.A.

17 16 15 14 13   6 5 4 3

R&H Cataloging Service
Consuegra, Claudio, 1958-   .
     Making Jesus my best friend:
baptism preparation for younger children,
by Claudio and Pamela Consuegra.

     Baptism—Juvenile works.   2. Bible—Catechisms,
question books, juvenile works.   I. Consuegra, Pamela, 1959-   .
II. Title.

          265.1

ISBN 978-0-8280-1836-4

Contents

Introduction

Several years ago I visited with an evangelist who was holding a series in my church. Later Pamela and I were heading to a home with several young children, and we talked about what our approach with the children might be. The evangelist had introduced me to a quote from Ellen G. White's book *Child Guidance:*

"Children of *eight, ten,* or *twelve* years are old enough to be addressed on the subject of personal religion. *Do not teach your children with reference to some future period when they shall be old enough to repent and believe the truth.* If properly instructed, very young children may have correct views of their state as sinners and of the way of salvation through Christ" (pp. 490, 491; italics supplied).

Several Bible study or baptismal preparation guides are geared to 10- to 12-year-olds and many others are available for teens, youth, and adults; but we have not found anything for the younger children: the 8- to 10-year-old kids.

We desire to help parents prepare children in this age group for a wonderful walk with their Best Friend, Jesus Christ, and to become ready for the ever-important step of baptism. We hope that this guide will be a useful, simple, fun way of preparing them for eternity, and that in the process you will get closer to your children and to the Father we all love and serve.

Yours because of Him,
Claudio and Pamela Consuegra

Instructions for Parents

Since one of the goals of this baptismal preparation guide is for parents and children to study together, we encourage one or both parents to spend time together with their children as they study each lesson.

Please follow these steps:

1. Begin with a short prayer, asking God to reveal what He wants you and your children to learn from this lesson.

2. Each lesson begins with a story; please read it together.

3. Each question can be answered by filling in the Bible text blanks. Unless otherwise specified, all texts are from the New King James Version of the Bible. (However, we have, at times, added a few words to the text to make it easier to understand. These words have brackets around them.)

4. After each question there is an explanatory statement; please read it together.

5. As a review, each lesson will have an activity; please do it together.

6. Close the study with prayer, using the message of the lesson as your conversation with God.

The B-i-b-l-e, God's Road Map

Remember to Pray

The Map

Daddy had a surprise for Michael and Matthew, and they were about to find out what it was.

"Now, Daddy; tell us now," said Matthew.

"OK," said Daddy. "I have brought you here because I have hidden a treasure somewhere in this park for you to find."

"But where do we start?" asked Michael.

"Well," said Daddy, "that is up to you."

Michael and Matthew looked at each other and quickly decided where to begin. They started by looking in the playground area. They looked in the seats of the swings. Nothing was there. They looked on the slide and around the seesaw. Nothing there, either. They looked around the merry-go-round and the basketball court, the tennis court, and the baseball field. They found no sign of any hidden treasure.

"Please, Daddy, can't you give us a hint?" said the boys together. "This is a *big* park, and we have already been looking for a while and have found nothing. Could you at least point us in the right direction?"

"Well," said Daddy, "I won't tell you where I have hidden the treasure, but I will give you something that may help you, if you use it correctly."

Daddy pulled out a piece of paper from his pocket and handed it to the boys. They held it in their hands and looked at it. It had drawings on it.

"Why, this looks like a swing set," said Matthew. "This is a slide, and here is a tree," said Michael.

"It is a map of the park," said Daddy. "And if you carefully follow the arrows and look in the place that is marked with an X, you will find the treasure that I have hidden for you."

Michael and Matthew looked at the drawing again and compared it to the park that they had just searched. They saw that the arrows pointed to a tree beside the playground. They ran to the tree and looked beside it. They saw an envelope stuffed into a hole in the tree.

"We found it," cried the boys. They opened the envelope and found airplane tickets inside. The tickets were for them to go and visit Grandma and Grandpa. They jumped for joy at the thought of spending a week with their grandparents.

That night for worship the family discussed the treasure hunt at the park. "Why was it so hard for you to find the treasure at first?" asked Daddy.

"Because we did not have any clues," said Matthew. "We did not know where to begin." "The map pointed you in the right direction," reminded Daddy. "It showed you which way to go."

Jesus gave all of us a treasure map. It points us in the right direction. It shows us which way to go. That treasure map is the Bible. Without it we can get lost.

God's Map for Our Lives

God has a map that helps us to know Him better and where He wants us to go. That map is the Bible.

Do you know how the Bible was written? Here's what one of its writers said:

☆ "Holy [men and women] of God _____ as they were moved [helped] by the Holy Spirit" (2 Peter 1:21).

☆ The Holy Spirit showed these people what God wanted them to know, and then helped them to write it all down correctly.

☆ The Bible is divided into two main parts: the Old Testament and the New Testament.

☆ Altogether there are 66 books: 39 in the Old Testament and 27 in the New Testament.

☆ Each book is divided into chapters, and each chapter into verses; that makes it easier to read.

Why would God give us these books all wrapped up into one?

Think and Do

Complete the words of the text below with these letters:

i l h w l a o

"The whole B___b___e was given to us by inspiration from God and is useful to teac___ us what is true and to make us realize what is ___rong in our lives; it straightens us out and he___ps us do what is right. It is God's w___y of making us well prepared at every point, fully equipped to do g___od to everyone" (2 Timothy 3:16, 17, TLB).

☺ ☺ ☺

The Bible has many stories—some sad, and some with a very happy ending.

Do you know why all these stories are in the Bible?

To find out, write in the blanks the words that are spelled backwards and underlined:

"These <u>sgniht</u> _____ happened . . .

as examples and were written <u>nwod</u> _____

as warnings for us" (1 Corinthians 10:11, NIV).

The Bible is God's road map for us. He gave us the Bible mainly to help us know Him better.

Jesus said, "These [the books of the Bible] are they which testify of <u>em</u> _____ " (John 5:39).

Remember, as you study the Bible,
to look for Jesus in all that it says.

Closing Activity ....

First fill in the blanks, and then use those words to complete the crossword puzzle.

ACROSS

1. "For _____ so loved the world that he gave his only Son" (John 3:16, RSV).
2. God helped the prophets who wrote the _____.
5. "If there is a prophet among you, I, the Lord, make Myself known to him in a _____" (Numbers 12:6).
7. "You are my _____ and my deliverer" (Psalm 40:17).
10. "But the Helper, the _____, whom the Father will send in My name, He will teach you all things, and bring to your remembrance all things that I said to you" (John 14:26).
11. A road _____ shows us where we are and where we need to go.

DOWN

1. "The Lord will _____ you continually" (Isaiah 58:11).
3. "God is _____" (1 John 4:8).
4. "The Lord your God will raise up for you a _____ like me from your midst, from your brethren. Him you shall hear" (Deuteronomy 18:15).
6. "And she will bring forth a Son, and you shall call His name_____, for He will save His people from their sins" (Matthew 1:21).
8. The letters and writings of the prophets that are in the Bible are divided into_____.
9. "And it shall come to pass afterward that I will pour out My Spirit on all flesh; your sons and your daughters shall prophesy, your old men shall dream _____, your young men shall see visions" (Joel 2:28).

Making Jesus My Best Friend

Don't forget to pray.

The Bad News and the Good News

Michael Learns Two Lessons

Today was a special day for Michael. It was his ninth birthday, and he had just received a new baseball bat, glove, and ball from his daddy. "Remember, Michael," said his daddy, "you will have to wait until we go to the park to play with this, because there are too many houses near here, and it will be easy to break a window. I will take you to the park tomorrow. You may play baseball there."

Michael walked outside holding his new gifts. *Tomorrow is a whole day away,* he thought as he held his baseball bat and rubbed his hand over the smooth wood. *Daddy can't expect me to wait an entire day to try out this bat. Why, I think I could hit a ball farther than any of my friends could.*

He laid the glove on the ground and started tossing the ball in the air with one hand as he held the bat in his other hand. *Just one hit,* he thought, *just one! I can't wait a whole day.* He threw the ball into the air and swung the bat. *Crack!* The ball soared high into the air. Michael smiled as he thought about what his friends would say if they could see him now. And then he heard a dreadful sound. It was the sound of glass breaking. The ball had sailed right through his living room window!

Holding the baseball in his hands, Daddy stepped out onto the porch and looked at Michael. Michael felt sad as he saw the disappointed look on Daddy's face. Daddy reached out his hand for Michael's new baseball bat. "I am so sorry, son. You chose to disobey, so now I will have to take away that new bat, glove, and ball." Michael sadly handed his precious birthday gifts to Daddy. Daddy sat down in the grass beside Michael. "I forgive you and love you so much," said Daddy. "My love for you will never change."

Every time Michael thought of his ninth birthday he remembered the two lessons that he had learned that day. He remembered the new baseball bat, glove, and ball that he had had to give up as a result of his disobedience. But most of all, he remembered how his daddy had forgiven him and would love him forever.

Think and Do

The Bad News

Fill in the missing words.

What is our problem?

"_____ have sinned and fall short of the glory of God" (Romans 3:23).

To fall short means that we didn't hit the target God has for us. The bad news is that every one of us has missed that target—we have sinned.

Another Bible writer explains that everyone who sins disobeys God's law. Disobedience is missing the target.

In the Olympic Games, the athlete who hits the target wins the prize—a gold medal. Just as an athlete wins a prize, a person who works gets a good reward—their wages. When we miss the target, we get a bad reward—death.

This is what one Bible writer says:

"For the _____ of sin is death" (Romans 6:23).

Here's how another Bible writer tells us what sin is:

"Whoever commits _____ also commits lawlessness [disobeys God's Ten Commandments], and sin is lawlessness" (1 John 3:4).

The Good News

Even though we have sinned (missed the target) and will get death as a result, God loves us so much that instead of death He wants to give us life (the prize for believing in Him).

Fill in the blanks for the rest of Romans 6:23:

"But the _____ of God is eternal _____ in Christ Jesus our Lord."

That's great news!
With Jesus we can hit the target!
We don't have to die!

Fill in the blanks to see what the Bible says about God's gift to us:

"God has given us eternal _____ , and this life is in His Son. [He or she] who has the _____ has life; [he or she] who does not have the Son of God does not have life. These things I have written to you who believe in the name of the Son of God, that you may know that you have eternal life, and that you may continue to _____ in the name of the Son of God" (1 John 5:11-13).

What do you have to do to have this gift of life?

"For God so loved the world that He _____ His only begotten Son, that whoever believes in _____ should not perish [die] but have everlasting _____" (John 3:16).

There is something else we can do to make sure that God forgives our sins:

"If we confess [tell God] our sins, _____ is faithful and just to forgive us our sins and to _____ us from _____ unrighteousness [all the bad things we have done]" (1 John 1:9).

Asking Jesus to forgive us when we have missed the target is very easy; it is as easy as going to the door when someone knocks on it, and opening it and inviting them in. Jesus says to us:

"_____ stand at the door and knock. If anyone hears My voice and _____ the door, I will come in to [him or her] and dine with [him or her], and [he or she] with Me" (Revelation 3:20).

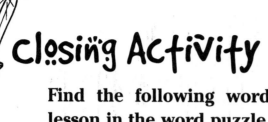

Closing Activity

Find the following words we have used in this lesson in the word puzzle.

SIN   PRIZE   GIFT   NEWS

GOD   BAD   DEATH   DIE

WAGES   JESUS   TARGET   LIFE

GOOD   REWARD   DOOR   BIBLE

```
          E O E                       U E U
        S E M W E               M T H T I
      E U S E A U H         T E N E A R E
    D P H V W G T S I N C H B L R E T D
    O N C N C E H N G I F T A K G E E J
    H U E C E S H I N E Y A D E E T E E
    V E S T F Y I K G O O D W T T N E F
    T D C G X B I B L E G D I E L W O R
    E E E E B G F L T L O N D E A T H S
    R J E S U S E J S D D R E W A R D O
    O R O A C T E O E O P S O I R E L A
      E P R I Z E E E O O B O I E T E
      R A L M R T O R S T E R T M
      A N E I V L J T N H H A
      T E L M I F X E F T
      O M F F V H W U
      E S E D E S
      T O S D
```

Don't forget to pray.

When Jesus Comes Back for Me

Remember to Pray

I Will Come Again

Daddy tried to explain it once again as Ashley's tears continued to fall. "Don't cry, Ashley," Daddy said. "I will be gone for only a little while. I have to go and get our new home ready. As soon as I have finished, I will come back again for you and Mommy. You wait for me, and one day soon you will see my red car drive in the driveway, and then we will go together to our new home." Ashley hugged Daddy one last time, and then he left. She stood at the window and waved a tearful goodbye.

When Ashley woke up the next morning, she asked, "Mommy, is today the day? Is today the day that Daddy will come to get us and take us to our new home?"

"Just keep watching, dear," said Mommy. "As soon as our new home is ready, then Daddy will come. Daddy needs to get our home ready, and we need to make sure that we are ready to leave when he gets here."

Ashley and Mommy worked together to get everything in the house packed up so that the boxes could be moved to the new house. Ashley helped pack her dolls, books, and her teddy bear. They wrapped the dishes, the glasses, and Mommy's crystal vase. They put towels, sheets, and blankets in boxes. There were boxes in every room of the house. Every drawer, cabinet, and closet was soon empty.

Ashley kept running to the window to look for Daddy's red car. "We are all ready now," said Ashley. "Is today the day that Daddy will come back to get us?"

"Just keep watching," said Mommy. "Daddy will be here as soon as our new home is ready."

Daddy had already been gone a whole week. Ashley went to the window and pulled up a chair. She sat in the chair and held her dolly. Her eyes were tired, but she knew that the red car would pull up soon. Daddy had said that he would come back again. He told her to get ready to move to their new house, and she had done that. She knew that Daddy would keep his promise.

Mommy came and sat beside Ashley. "Let's read a story while we wait," Mommy said. Mommy opened Ashley's Bible story book and started to read. "Jesus told His disciples, 'I am going to get a new home ready for you. And I will come again soon and get you so that you can live with Me forever.'"

"Hey," said Ashley, "that story sounds like our family. Daddy has gone to get a new home ready for us—just like Jesus! And Daddy said that he would come back again soon—just like Jesus!" Out of the corner of her eye Ashley saw a flash of red and knew that it was Daddy's car. She ran and opened the door and jumped right into Daddy's arms. "Oh, Daddy," said Ashley. "You kept your promise and came back for us. We waited and watched for you. You have a new home ready for us, and we are ready to go and live with you. Now we will wait, watch, and get ready for Jesus to come and take us to live in our new home in heaven." Mommy hugged Daddy with a twinkle in her eye.

Jesus Comes Back

Before Jesus went back to heaven, He gave His friends very good news. **Fill in the blanks and read His promise** in John 14:1-3.

"Let not your _____ be troubled; you believe in God, believe also in Me. In My Father's _____ are many mansions; if it were not so, I would have told you. I go to prepare a place for _____ . And if I go and prepare a place for you, I will come _____ and receive you to Myself; that where I am, there _____ may be also."

Jesus wants us to be with Him in His house in heaven. He has been preparing a special place for you and your family, and one day soon He will come back and take us there. We don't know exactly when Jesus will come back for us. That is why we need to do some preparation and be ready all the time. Studying these lessons is part of your preparation.

What Else Should We Do?

"W_____ therefore, and p_____

always" (Luke 21:36).

Watch for news that He's coming back, and pray every day.

We Can't Miss It!

Do you know how many people will see Jesus when He comes back? Check it out!

"Every _____will see Him" (Revelation 1:7).

All of us will see Him! When He comes back, it will be bright like lightning and loud like thunder.

And Jesus doesn't come back alone. Fill in the blanks to see who else comes with Him.

"When the Son of Man comes in His glory, and _____ the holy _____ with Him, then He will sit on the throne of His glory" (Matthew 25:31).

Just imagine that! Jesus needs the help of all His angels to pick up all His friends from all over the world and take them back to heaven to live with Him.

But what about the people who have died? Jesus has great news! He does not forget those who died believing in Him!

To read this exciting news, write the letter *a* inside the stars ☆, *e* inside the squares ▢, *o* inside the diamonds ◇, and *i* inside the Stars of David ✡.

"For the L◇rd himself will come down from h▢☆ven with a mighty shout and with the soul-stirring cry of the ☆rchangel and the great trumpet-call of G◇d. And the believers who are d▢☆d will be the f✡rst to r✡se to m▢▢t the L◇rd" (1 Thessalonians 4:16, TLB).

Do the same in the next passage to discover what will happen next to us who are alive when Jesus comes back.

"Then we who are still ☆l✡v ☐ and remain on the earth will be caught up with th☐m [the dead that came back to life] in the cl◇uds to meet the L◇rd in the ☆ ✡r and remain with him f◇r☐v☐r"

(1 Thessalonians 4:17, TLB).

After Jesus comes back, there won't be any more sadness, or pain, or sickness, or death. Won't that be great? That's why we should be happy that Jesus is coming soon!

closing Activity ....

Write a list of people you would like Jesus to take to heaven with you when He comes back.

My special list of people:

_____

_____

_____

_____

_____

Pray every day for the people on your list so that they too will want to come along.

Don't forget to pray.

Using the key below, change the symbols into letters to reveal two special verses about the second coming of Jesus.

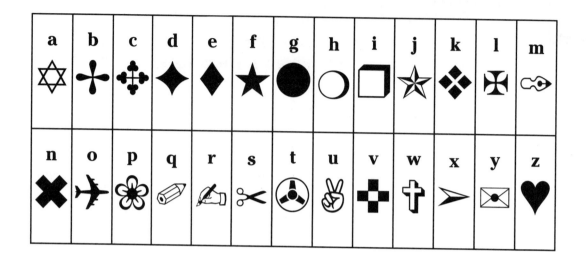

a	b	c	d	e	f	g	h	i	j	k	l	m
✡	✚	✛	◆	◆	★	●	○	◻	☆	❖	✠	⚷

n	o	p	q	r	s	t	u	v	w	x	y	z
✖	✈	✿	✎	✍	✂	⊙	✌	✚	✝	➤	✉	♥

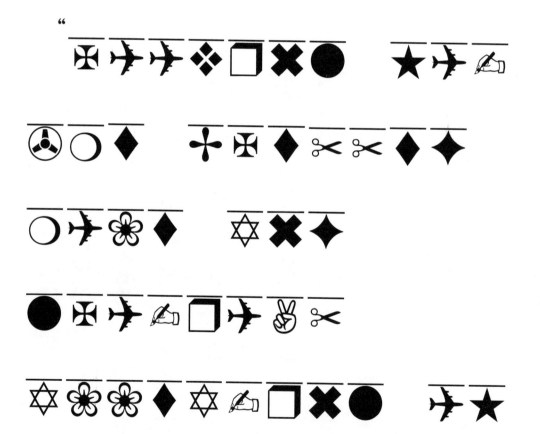

"Looking for the blessed hope and glorious appearing of

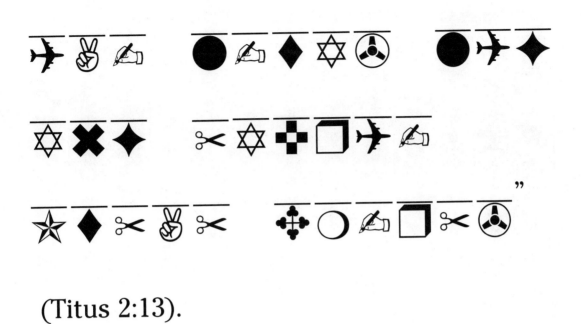

(Titus 2:13).

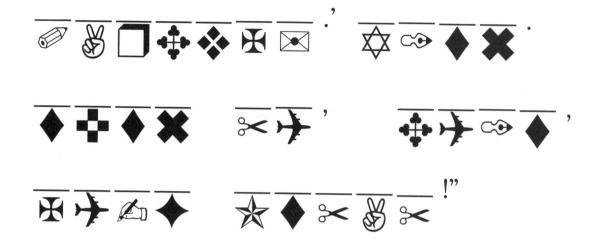

(Revelation 22:20).

Don't forget to pray.

Resting With My Friend, Jesus

A Special Day

Matthew and Michael sat on the bed watching Daddy get ready. He had come home from work, changed his dirty work clothes, and taken a shower. Michael had helped Daddy rub shaving cream all over his face and shave. And now Daddy was getting all dressed up in a suit and tie. It was Tuesday night, and the boys knew that it was a special night in their house. It was the night that Mommy and Daddy spent together. A babysitter was coming to watch them while their parents went out.

"Why do you always go out with Mommy?" asked Michael.

"Well," said Daddy, "it is our special evening together. Here, sit beside me on the bed. I want to show you something." Daddy was holding a small black book in his hands. He opened it up and began turning the pages. "This is my appointment book. I write everything in it that I will do each day. It helps me keep track of the time of meetings and special events. It keeps me organized. Take a look at today, Tuesday." Daddy turned the page, and the boys looked at Tuesday. They read, "7:00 p.m.—A Date With My Wife!"

"Wow!" said Matthew, "Mommy's name is in your book. Look, I see Mommy's name on every Tuesday."

"That's right," said Daddy. "Tuesday is a special day. I have made a promise that I will spend every Tuesday evening with your mommy. We forget about work, and we spend time with each other. We talk and share things. It helps our love for each other to grow even stronger when we spend our special day together."

"What else do you have in your book, Daddy?" asked Matthew. Daddy handed the little book to the boys and gave them permission to look carefully at it while he finished getting dressed. "Look," said Michael as he flipped through the pages, "you have another special day in your book that you have marked every week. You have the same words written on every Saturday. It says, 'A Date With My Best Friend—Jesus!' What does that mean?"

"Well," said Daddy, "it means that I have a special appointment every week with my Best Friend. You see, once every week my Best Friend has asked me to reserve the day just for Him. We spend time together. We talk and share things. It helps our love for each other to grow even stronger when we spend our special day together. I look forward to that day every week. It is my time with Jesus. He has that day written in His calendar too. He plans every week to meet with us on that day. He has our names written in His book, and He looks forward to our appointment with Him."

The boys hugged Daddy and Mommy goodbye, and they ran to get a piece of paper. They had plans that Tuesday night. They wanted the babysitter to help them make their own "date book," and they wanted to write down their first appointment—every Saturday with their Best Friend, Jesus!

Making Jesus My Best Friend

Think and Do  ....

God's Special Day With Me

God created Adam and Eve and then married them. **Fill in the blanks to see what His wedding gift for them was and what He did.**

"And on the seventh day _____ ended His work which He had done, and He _____ on the seventh day from all His work which He had done. Then God _____ the _____ day and _____ it, because in it He rested from all His work which God had created and made" (Genesis 2:2, 3).

Later God reminded Moses and the Israelites to keep this special day, the seventh day, which is also called the Sabbath.

"Remember the Sabbath _____ , to keep it holy. Six days you shall labor and do all your _____ , but the seventh day is the Sabbath of the Lord _____ God" (Exodus 20:8-10).

The Sabbath is a special day of joy, and God wants us to spend it with Him. He wants us to have great fun on this day.

Use the words in the following list to complete the text.

breaking	delight	idle	please
holy	own	joy	

"If you keep your feet from b_____ the Sabbath and from doing as you p_____ on my holy day, if you call the Sabbath a d_____ and the Lord's h_____ day honorable, and if you honor it by not going your o_____ way and not doing as you please or speaking i_____ words, then you will find your j_____ in the Lord" (Isaiah 58:13, 14, NIV).

Jesus knew how special the Sabbath is. **Read the following text and then write why He went to His church on Sabbath.**

"So He came to Nazareth, where He had been brought up. And as His custom was, He went into the synagogue on the Sabbath day, and stood up to read" (Luke 4:16).

It was His _____ .

The Sabbath is our special date with God. And God wants to spend that special time with us forever. The following text tells us that we will even keep the Sabbath in heaven and forever on the earth when God makes it new.

"From new moon to new moon, and from sabbath to sabbath, all flesh shall come to worship before me, says the Lord" (Isaiah 66:23, NRSV).

You can begin to enjoy this special time with God this week starting on Friday evening, when the sun goes down.

closing Activity

Begin at the top arrow and come out at the bottom arrow. You will know you are on the right path when you collect the five words to complete God's invitation to us below.

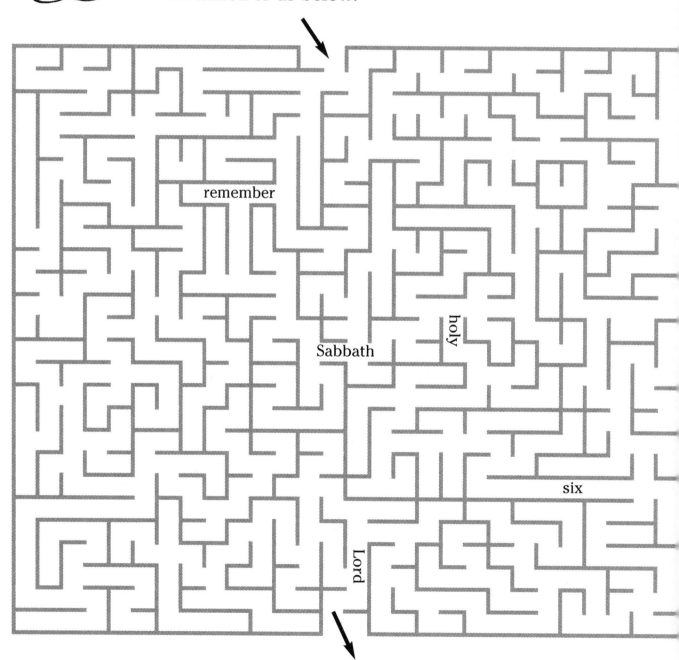

Making Jesus My Best Friend

_____ to keep the

_____ day _____ . You

can do all your work in _____ days,

but the Sabbath day belongs to the

_____ .

Don't forget to pray.

All of Me for Him

Remember to Pray

Story

I Belong to Jesus!

It was almost Christmas! Ashley should have felt excited, but instead she was sad. In church that morning the teacher had told the class that Christmas was Jesus' birthday and that they were going to have a birthday party for Jesus next week. Birthday parties meant cake and ice cream, but they also meant presents. That was why she was so sad. What could she possibly take to a birthday party for Jesus? What could she give Him that He did not already have? After all, He had made the whole world. She thought and thought. Jesus deserved something really special, but what would that be? This was really a problem.

Ashley kept thinking about it all day in school on Monday. She could hardly concentrate on her math problems. She didn't feel like playing jump rope with the other girls at recess. She was sure that they would all have a really neat present to bring to the party, and she had nothing. She didn't feel like eating her dinner that night. She wasn't very hungry.

When it was time for family worship that night, Mommy looked at Ashley and said, "I can tell that you are upset about something. Did you have a bad day at school today?"

"Not really," said Ashley.

"Are you sick?" asked Daddy.

"Not really," said Ashley.

"Then why do you look so sad?" asked Mommy.

"Well," said Ashley, "we are going to have a birthday party for Jesus in our class next week at church, and I don't know what to take as a gift. The teacher said she wanted all of us to think about a special gift to bring for Jesus. I have been thinking and thinking, but I just can't think of anything that I can take. Jesus has everything already. I am sure that the other kids will bring really good gifts, and I won't have anything. I guess I can't go to the party."

"H'mmm, it sounds like you have a pretty big problem," said Daddy. "But I think that I can help you find an answer. When we have a problem, Jesus will help us. And I think that if we look in the Bible, we'll find that He can help us with this one. In Romans 12:1 it says, 'Present your bodies a living sacrifice.'"

"What does that mean?" asked Ashley.

Mommy answered, "A sacrifice is something that you give God. The text tells us to present our bodies as a sacrifice to Him. That means that we should give ourselves to Jesus."

"I think I have an idea for the party now," said Ashley, "Thank you, Mommy and Daddy."

The day of the birthday party finally arrived. The teacher asked the class, one by one, to show what their gift was and to tell about it. Michael had brought a stack of cards that he had made to take to the children in the hospital. The teacher said that was a good gift for Jesus. Matthew had a basket filled with soap, shampoo, and lotion to take to an older person in a nursing home. The teacher said that his gift would make Jesus smile. Michelle had a plate filled with homemade cookies that she was going to take to a new neighbor that had just moved in. The teacher liked her gift, too. And then it was Ashley's turn. She was scared because she didn't have any gift that was wrapped up.

"You are next, Ashley," said the teacher. "What did you bring for Jesus' birthday gift?" One little boy started laughing because he thought that Ashley had forgotten to bring a present to the birthday party. Ashley thought about what Mommy and Daddy had said, and then she stood up.

"Well," Ashley said. "I have thought about this all week. At first I was sad, because I didn't know what to bring. Then I read in the Bible that we are to give our bodies as a sacrifice to Jesus. So I am bringing myself to this party. I think the best gift we can give to Jesus is ourselves. I am the gift for Jesus today."

The teacher smiled a big smile and said, "You have brought the best gift, Ashley. The most important gift that we can ever give to Jesus is ourselves. We need to give everything that we have to Him."

"Happy birthday, Jesus," said Ashley, smiling.

Think and Do ·······················

All of Me for Him

God gives us everything we have—life, health, home, and many other things. He does that because He loves us.

When we love Him, we will want to give Him something, too. Here are four things you can give God that would make Him very happy.

My Time

While we are always God's, He wants us to spend a special day with Him; do you remember what that day is called?

Find the text, and fill in the missing word.

"The _____" (Mark 2:27).

My Talents

"Whatever you do, do well" (Ecclesiastes 9:10, TLB).

Some people have the talent of singing. Others can paint beautiful pictures. Can you think of other talents that people can use for God? **Write your ideas on the lines below:**

_____   _____   _____

_____   _____   _____

_____   _____   _____

_____   _____   _____

What are your talents? **Write them on the lines provided:**

_____   _____   _____

_____   _____   _____

My Treasure

Look up the following text in your Bible and fill in the missing word.

"All the _____ . . . is the Lord's" (Leviticus 27:30).

The tithe is used to pay the wages for pastors, teachers, and missionaries all over the world. The tithe is one part of every 10. **Circle the tithe of the pennies, nickels, dimes, and quarters.**

My Body Temple

How can we make God very happy?

Look the text up on your Bible, and fill in the missing words.

"Whether you _____ or _____, or whatever you _____, do all to the glory of _____" (1 Corinthians 10:31).

Why do you think we should take care of our bodies? **To find out, write in the blanks the words that are spelled backwards and underlined:**

"Haven't you yet learned that your <u>ydob</u> _____ is the <u>emoh</u> _____ of the Holy Spirit God gave <u>uoy</u> _____ , and that he <u>sevil</u> _____ within you? Your own body does not belong to you" (1 Corinthians 6:19, TLB).

We wouldn't think of throwing garbage inside a church. Well, let's not put any garbage in God's temple—our bodies.

What are some good things God told us we should eat?

Read the Bible verse and fill in the missing words.

"And God said, 'See, I have given you every _____ that yields _____ which is on the face of all the earth, and every _____ whose _____ yields seed; to you it shall be for _____.'" (Genesis 1:29).

What are your favorite foods? **Write some on the lines provided.**

_____ _____ _____

_____ _____ _____

_____ _____ _____

Many years later God told His people that if they chose to eat meat they should make sure it was the kind approved by Him.

Read Leviticus 11 and then make a list of some of the animals that God doesn't want to us to eat because they are unclean.

_____   _____   _____

_____   _____   _____

_____   _____   _____

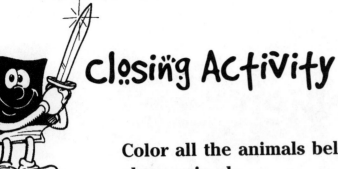

closing Activity

Color all the animals below and then circle all the clean animals.

Don't forget to pray.

Wheñ Life Eñds

Remember to Pray

Asleep Until Jesus Comes

Michael and Matthew were on their way to see Grandpa. He had been sick and in the hospital for a long time, and he had telephoned and asked Daddy to bring them in to see him. He wanted to talk with them.

When they arrived at the hospital, Grandpa was sitting up, in bed, waiting for them. "Come in, boys," said Grandpa. "I have been waiting to talk to you." The boys ran over and gave Grandpa a big hug. Daddy helped the boys put a chair close to Grandpa's bed, and they sat down.

Grandpa began, "Boys, the doctor came to see me today. He got the results back from a test that I had done. He told me that this body of mine is beginning to wear out. He said that I will soon go to sleep."

"What do you mean, Grandpa? If you are tired, we can leave so that you can take a nap," said Michael.

"No," said Grandpa, "I don't think you understand. The doctor said that I won't have long to live."

"Do you mean that you are going to die?" asked Matthew.

"Well," said Grandpa, "I would rather look at death in the way that Jesus taught us. That is why I wanted you boys to come here today. I wanted to explain it to you myself. I do not want you boys to be sad."

"You see, my body is old and tired. Jesus has given me many wonderful years of life. It is just time for me to rest. I will soon close my eyes and go to sleep."

"Why do you keep saying that? Why do you say that you are going to sleep?" asked Matthew.

Grandpa answered, "Well, in the Bible that is what Jesus called death. He said that death is like a sleep. He said that one day soon He will come back and wake up all those who loved Him before they died. He will wake them up and take them to live with Him forever in heaven. You see, death is just like a sleep. When I close my eyes and go to sleep, it is only for a little while. I want you boys to remember that one day soon Jesus will wake me up, and then I will go with you to live with Him forever.

"When you feel sad, I want you to remember our talk today. Think about the promise Jesus made and the place that He is preparing for us in heaven. You can believe His promises. He is my very Best Friend, and I want you to make Him your Best Friend too. I can't wait to open my eyes after my sleep and see my Best Friend's face coming to take me home to live with Him forever. I will never get sick in heaven. Why, I'll even be able to run a race with you boys, and I may even beat you. I love you, boys; and I am looking forward to spending eternity with Jesus and with you."

Soon after that visit the boys were at Grandpa's funeral. Grandpa had gone to sleep, just as he said he would. They missed Grandpa, but they thought about that day he called them into the hospital. They remembered his words to them. When they felt sad, they thought about the day that Grandpa had told them about. They imagined what it would be like when Jesus woke up Grandpa from his sleep, and they imagined the race that Grandpa would run with them in heaven. Would Grandpa really be able to beat them? They couldn't wait to find out.

Think and Do

How Life Began

On the sixth day of Creation God made the first two people. This is how it happened:

Fill in the missing words.

"And the Lord _____ formed man of the dust of the ground, and breathed into his nostrils the breath of _____ ; and man became a living _____" (Genesis 2:7).

Adam became a human being when God made him from a lump of clay and then breathed life into his lungs.

When Life Ends

At the moment of death the reverse of what happened at Creation takes place. **Read about this process in the next text and fill in the missing words:**

"Then the _____ will return to the earth as it was, and the spirit will return to _____ who gave it" (Ecclesiastes 12:7).

Death is not scary. Jesus says that being dead is like being asleep. When His friend Lazarus died, Jesus said:

"Our friend Lazarus _____ , but I go that I may wake him up" (John 11:11).

And just so that no one might misunderstand what He meant, then Jesus said:

"Lazarus is _____ " (John 11:14).

Since the dead are asleep, they don't know anything that's happening now. They are not suffering or in pain. And they can't scare us, either.

When Life Begins Again

The good news from the Bible is that even if people die, they will not be dead forever.

The Bible tells us what will happen the day that Jesus comes back to take us to heaven with Him:

Fill in the missing words from the Scripture written below.

"The _____ in Christ will rise first. Then _____ who are alive and remain shall be caught up together with them in the clouds to meet the Lord in the air. And thus we shall always be with the Lord" (1 Thessalonians 4:16, 17).

It's wonderful to know that even if people we love die and we don't see them for a while, one day, when Jesus comes back, they will come back to life, and we will be together again. That will be the best family reunion ever!

Let's plan to be there!

closing Activity ....

Find the following words we have used in this lesson in the word puzzle.

JESUS   GROUND   FAMILY   FOREVER

DEAD   DEATH   DUST   CREATION

HUMAN   SCARE   END   BEGINS

BREATH   BEING   SCARY   GOD

CLAY

SLEEP

REUNION

HEAVEN

LIFE

```
            E E H N C I B W
            R A R B E I N G
            T T W H I N K N
            F A M I L Y N Y
            T S C A R Y R I
D R G N E A A E T E F C O B A E T M
E E R D C C C S B N E R N R E E G I
A U O S L E E P E I H E D E A T H E
D N U D A A O A G A O A U A I A N N
Q I N X Y H E Y I E S T U T P R F D
O O D E D U S T N U E I U H C D D S
D N G O D M V A S R L O S J E S U S
O E E I N A G Z T R I N S P T N S O
            N A H H S F A C
            E E I C A E T A
            N F O R E V E R
            F H E A V E N E
            P A N Y E C T F
```

Don't forget to pray.

My Friend, the Judge

Remember to Pray

Story

My Best Friend, the Judge

Michael was so excited. He was holding his new puppy. It was a special birthday gift. At first he did not know what to name his puppy; but every time he stood up to go anywhere, that little puppy would be following right beside him. Because of this, he had decided to name his puppy Shadow.

Shadow and Michael soon became best of friends. When Michael got home from school, Shadow was wagging his tail, waiting for him. Shadow and Michael would play together in the yard. Michael would even read a story from his reading book to Shadow. Michael took good care of Shadow by always making sure that food and water were in his dishes. He would also give Shadow a bath to keep him clean. As Shadow grew and became bigger, their friendship grew also.

One day the whole family was working to get things ready for company. Daddy was working outside in the yard, Mommy was doing the laundry and mopping the floors, and Michael was cleaning his room.

Shadow wanted to play, but the entire family was busy getting ready for visitors. "Not now," said Michael. "I have to get this room cleaned up. My cousin will be here tonight to stay with me, and my room needs to be nice and clean."

"I'm sorry, Shadow," said Mommy. "I have to finish washing all this laundry. You go outside. I can't play now."

"I'm busy right now," said Daddy. "I have to finish planting these rosebushes."

Poor Shadow! No one had time for him. He went and lay down in the corner of the yard. Just then a bright-yellow butterfly flew by Shadow. That was the most interesting thing he had seen all day. Shadow jumped up and started chasing the butterfly. The butterfly flew right over Daddy's rosebushes, and Shadow followed. As Daddy watered his roses with the garden hose, Shadow ran right through Daddy's roses. And the water that was meant for the rosebushes went all over Shadow.

"Stop, Shadow," yelled Daddy, but Shadow's eyes stayed on that bright-yellow butterfly, and he kept going.

Mommy opened the door to see what all the commotion was about and—wouldn't you know it?—that bright-yellow butterfly went right past Mommy and into the house. And of course Shadow followed and was in the house and past Mommy before she could shut the door.

"Stop," Mommy called. But Shadow's muddy paws ran right over Mommy's clean, shiny floors. Shadow didn't stop there. He kept going and passed through the laundry room and trotted through the stack of clean clothes that Mommy had just folded. Shadow raced on toward Michael's room with Daddy and Mommy close behind. He heard them both screaming at him, so he jumped up onto Michael's bed and hid under the covers. Michael picked up his muddy puppy and headed outside.

After Michael had given Shadow a bath, Mommy and Daddy called a family meeting. They had to decide what would have to be done with the disobedient puppy. "Well," said Daddy, "this puppy has been very naughty. He caused a lot of trouble today for everyone in this family. He trampled my rosebushes."

"He got mud all over my clean floors and dirtied all my clean laundry," said Mommy.

"He made a big mess," said Daddy, "and did not obey even when we told him to stop. Shadow cannot be a part of our family if he cannot obey."

Shadow had his head on Michael's lap. Michael rubbed his clean fur. He just couldn't imagine losing his best friend. Michael wiped a tear from his eye and said, "Mommy and Daddy, I know that Shadow was naughty. He did not obey. When you asked him to stop, he just kept going and got into a lot of trouble. He made a mess both inside and outside the house. He created a problem for every member of this family. He does not deserve to be a member of this family. But I love him, and he loves me. He is my friend. I will always love him, no matter what he does."

Daddy looked at Michael and saw Shadow licking Michael's hands as they stroked Shadow's fur. Daddy said, "Michael, you just defended your puppy. That makes you his lawyer. Now I want you to decide what to do with him. That will make you his judge, also."

Michael thought about the puppy, the puppy's naughty behavior, how much he loved his puppy, and then said, "I will go with Shadow to a dog obedience school. I will work with him to help him obey. With us working together, Shadow can stay in our family. That is my decision."

Holding Michael close and patting Shadow's head, Daddy said, "Shadow, you are a fortunate little puppy. Your best friend, Michael, was your lawyer and your judge. How could you lose?"

Making Jesus My Best Friend

Think and Do ·····································

God's Sanctuary

Fill in the blanks where indicated.

God told Moses to build a sanctuary (like a church) that would be like the one God built in heaven. In Moses' sanctuary there were priests (like pastors today) who presented offerings to God. But in the sanctuary in heaven it is Jesus who is our High Priest.

"We have such a High Priest, who is seated at the _____ hand of the throne of the Majesty in the heavens, a Minister of the sanctuary and of the _____ tabernacle [sanctuary] which the Lord erected [built], and not man" (Hebrews 8:1, 2).

Many years ago God told Daniel that one day the sanctuary in heaven would have to be cleansed from all the bad things we have done—all our sins. The cleansing of the sanctuary is also called the day of judgment.

In the book of Revelation, God shows one angel that has a very special message for everyone in the world. **What does he say about the judgment?**

"The hour of His judgment has _____" (Revelation 14:7).

According to a prophecy of Daniel (8:14), and this message of the first angel, God's judgment began in 1844 (a long, long time ago), and it is still going on—but soon it will come to an end.

God's Judgment

Just as it is in the courtrooms on earth, there are several people who participate in the judgment.

Look up the following texts and write down who each of the participants is and what law is used in God's judgment:

✫ The Judge (Mark 1:9-11; John 5:22)

_____

✫ The accuser (Revelation 12:9, 10)

_____

⭐ Our Defense Attorney (1 John 2:1)

_____

[*advocate* is another word for defense attorney or defender]

⭐ The law used (James 2:8-12)

_____

[the Ten Commandments]

The bad news is that the devil accuses us before the Judge. But the good news is that Jesus is both our Judge and our Defender! We can't lose our case when Jesus, our Best Friend, is defending us!

Since our Best Friend, Jesus, is defending us, should we be afraid to come to God's judgment?

Fill in the missing words. You may have to look up the verses in your Bible.

"Let us therefore _____ boldly [with confidence] to the throne of grace, that we may obtain mercy and find grace to help in _____ of need" (Hebrews 4:16).

We can look forward to the judgment, because soon after it is finished, Jesus will come back to take us to heaven to be with Him.

Closing Activity

Black out the squares in which you find the following letters:

B K Q V X Z

Now use the letters that remain to write the words on the lines on the next page.

W	B	K	O	Q	R	V	X	Z	B	S	K
Q	V	H	X	Z	B	I	K	Q	V	P	X
Z	T	B	K	H	Q	V	E	X	Z	B	L
O	K	Q	R	V	X	Z	D	B	K	F	Q
V	X	O	Z	B	R	K	Q	V	T	X	Z
B	H	K	Q	V	E	X	Z	B	H	K	Q
V	X	Z	O	B	K	U	Q	V	R	X	Z
O	B	K	Q	F	V	X	Z	H	B	K	Q
V	I	X	Z	B	S	K	Q	V	J	X	Z
B	K	U	Q	V	D	X	Z	G	B	K	M
Q	E	V	N	X	Z	T	B	H	K	Q	A
S	V	X	C	Z	B	O	K	Q	M	V	E

__ __ __ __ __ __ __ __ __ __

__ __ __ __ , __ __ __ __ __

__ __ __ __ __ __ __ __

__ __ __ __ __ __ __ __ __

__ __ __ __ .

Don't forget to pray.

Gifts for Everybody

Remember to Pray

Story

God's Special Gift to Ellen

It was time for family worship. Ashley snuggled close to Mommy as she settled down to listen to a special story that Mommy had promised for that night. She had promised to tell Ashley a story about a little girl whose name was Ellen. Mommy began her story.

Ellen was born a long time ago, in the year 1827, in the state of Maine. When Ellen was 9 years old, a terrible accident happened. She was on the way home from school when an angry girl began following Ellen and saying mean and ugly words. Ellen turned around to see how close the girl was, and just then the girl threw a stone at Ellen. The stone hit Ellen right in the face. She fell down, unconscious. Ellen's twin sister and a friend carried Ellen home. Her face and clothes were covered with blood. Everyone thought that little Ellen would die. She did not wake up for three weeks. The stone had broken Ellen's nose and even changed the way her face looked. It had also damaged Ellen's eyes. Ellen was sick for a very long time. She had to stop going to school and study at home.

Even though this terrible thing happened to Ellen, God was watching after her. He still loved her and was taking care of her. Ellen's favorite book became the Bible. She loved to read the stories, and she also loved to spend time in nature. She came to know Jesus as her Best Friend.

When Ellen was 17 years old, something very special happened to her. God had a plan for Ellen. He had a special work that she was to do for Him. He gave her a gift to help her with His plan for her life. Ellen had a vision. A vision is like a dream. Ellen had her first vision at 17 years of age, and she had many more after that. God had chosen Ellen to be His messenger. He would give her messages in these visions. These messages helped to encourage God's people. They helped God's people know the truth and follow Jesus. It was Ellen's job to tell others about these visions and to write down the messages from God.

God gave Ellen strength and health, and for the rest of her life she used this special gift that He had given her. She lived to be 87 years of age. She wrote many thousands of pages filled with words that Jesus gave her. It was His special gift to her, and she used that gift to serve Him.

Mommy looked at Ashley, still snuggled on her lap, and said, "Ashley, God has given you special gifts too. These gifts are sometimes called talents. He gives each of us special talents. Just like Ellen, we should always choose to use those gifts to serve Him."

"Do you mean that I have special gifts too?" asked Ashley.

"Yes," said Mommy. Your gifts may be different from Ellen's, and my gifts may be different from yours, but God gives all of us special gifts."

Ashley thought for a moment about what her special gift might be. "My teacher says that I am a good friend. She says that I care about people in my class and that I am kind. Is that a gift from Jesus?"

Mommy hugged Ashley and said, "Yes, Ashley, that is a very special gift, and you must always use that gift to serve Jesus."

"I will," said Ashley, "I will use my special gift from God, just as Ellen used hers."

Think and Do

God's Special Gift

God loves us so much that He wants to give us a very special gift. **Read the text and write down the words to complete it.**

"If you then, being evil, know how to give good _____ to your children, how much more will _____ heavenly Father give the Holy Spirit to those who _____ Him!" (Luke 11:13).

☺ ☺ ☺

When we receive the Holy Spirit, we are like a tree with lots of good fruit. **Read Galatians 5:22, 23, and then write down the different fruit on the tree.**

And with the Holy Spirit come a lot of other gifts. **Read the following texts and then write down some of the gifts that the Holy Spirit gives us:** 1 Corinthians 12:1, 7-11; Ephesians 4:11-13.

_____ _____ _____

_____ _____ _____

_____ _____ _____

_____ _____ _____

One of those special gifts God gave His church through the Holy Spirit is the gift of prophecy. Prophets are people whom God chooses to show things about Himself and about His plans for our future. Prophets can be men or women, old or young.

God talks to prophets in two different ways. You can read about them in Joel 2:28 and then write them in the spaces below.

✪ 1. Through _____

✪ 2. Through _____

In the days before the return of Jesus, God tells us about His special people. He tells us that to recognize His people we have to see if they keep the Ten Commandments and have prophets (Revelation 12:17; 19:10; 22:9).

Making Jesus My Best Friend

The Seventh-day Adventist Church teaches people to obey the Ten Commandments. God also blessed this church with the gift of prophecy in the person of Ellen G. White. These two things—and others you will learn as you study your Bible and your Sabbath school lesson—make it clear that the Adventist people have been chosen as God's church for the last days.

Isn't it wonderful that God tells us what we need to know and that He also sends us such people as the prophets to help us?

God's gifts are always good!

Closing Activity ··························

Find the words we used in this lesson in the Gifts of the Spirit Tree on the next page.

on the next page.

LOVE	FRUIT	JOY
GIFTS	GOD	PEACE
KINDNESS	GOODNESS	HEALINGS
FAITHFULNESS	WISDOM	TONGUES
GENTLENESS	MIRACLES	TEACHERS
SELF-CONTROL	PROPHECY	APOSTLES
HOLY SPIRIT	PASTORS	
KNOWLEDGE	EVANGELISTS	
LONGSUFFERING	ELLEN G. WHITE	

Making Jesus My Best Friend

```
W T A L E V A N G E L I S T S E O E
I O P P M F A I T H F U L N E S S N
S N O R I N L S H L O V E P C O W G
D G S O R H O K O G S S L A F Z P I
O U T P A L N N L O E G L S R A E F
M E L H C R G O Y D L O E T U E A T
L S E E L T S W S G F O N O I P C S
  F S C E E U L P E C D G R T R E
  T Y S A F E I N O N W S N E
      C F D R T N E H
      H E G I L T S I
      E R E T E R S T
      R I N L N O N E
      S N S T E L J P
      C G N H S W O Y
      E L W P S M Y D
      K I N D N E S S
      H E A L I N G S
```

Don't forget to pray.

Gifts for Everybody | 71

God's Special People

Remember to Pray

A Sweet Smell

It was Matthew and Michael's favorite time of day. It was worship time, and Mommy and Daddy always made it a special time together. Tonight they were especially curious because Mommy had a basket with her. The boys couldn't see what was inside, because there was a cover on top.

Mommy took a blindfold out of the basket and said, "We are going to play a game tonight. You will take turns putting on the blindfold. Then I have different things for you to smell. I would like for you to tell me what the smell makes you think of. Now, who wants to go first?"

"I do," said Michael. Mommy put the blindfold on Michael, and then she took the first item out of the basket. She held it close to Michael's nose so he could smell it. "Mmmm, it smells like apple. It reminds me of Great-grandma's apple pie," said Michael. Mommy showed him what it was—a small bowl of cooked apples.

Matthew was next. He put on the blindfold and sniffed. "That smells just like Grandpa," said Matthew. He took off the blindfold and saw a bottle of Grandpa's cologne. Both boys held their nose as the top came off of the next container. "That smells like the garbage," said both boys together. They were not sure what it was, but it was certainly rotten. Their reaction to the smell was not pleasant, so Mommy quickly put it away.

The next smell really made Michael hungry. It smelled just like Mommy's lemon cookies. They were the boys' favorite.

Then Daddy opened the Bible and read a verse from it. The verse said, "We are the sweet smell of Christ" (see 2 Corinthians 2:15).

Daddy said, "What do you think that means, boys? What does it mean to be a sweet smell?"

"I think I know," said Michael. "Most smells tonight made us think of good things. The smell made us think of people we love. But there was one smell that was terrible. That smell made us think of a place that was not pleasant. If we are like a smell, then we need to make sure that we have a sweet smell."

"Yes," said Michael, "when people think of us they need to think of pleasant things. When others think about us, we do not want them to think of us the way the rotten garbage smelled."

Daddy said, "That's right, boys. We are God's children. We are children of the King of the universe. We need to be different from those who don't believe in Jesus. We need to act like a child of the King in all that we do and say. Everything that we do and say is like a "smell." That aroma, or smell, comes from knowing Jesus and being a part of His special people. We need to make sure that we are the sweet smell of Christ, just as the verse says.

Think and Do

You Are Special

God loves you! You are very special to Him! Look how many different ways He says that. **Read the texts and fill in the missing words.**

"But _____ are a chosen generation, a royal priesthood, a holy nation, His _____ special people" (1 Peter 2:9).

Because we are special, God wants us to be different from those who don't believe in Him.

☆ We are different in what we eat (lesson 5).

☆ We are different in that we worship God as our Creator by keeping the Sabbath (lesson 4).

☆ We are also different in how we dress. How we look on the outside should not be the most important thing in our life.

To find out what God thinks is really important; write in the blanks the words that are spelled backwards and underlined:

"Don't be concerned about the outward ytuaeb _____ that depends on jewelry, or beautiful clothes, or riah _____ arrangement. Be beautiful inside, in your straeh _____ , with the lasting charm of a eltneg _____ and quiet spirit which is so precious to God. That kind of peed _____ beauty was seen in the saintly women of old" (1 Peter 3:3-5, TLB).

To find out how God wants us to dress on the outside, write the letter *a* inside the stars ☆, *e* inside the squares ☐, *o* inside the diamonds ◇, and *i* inside the Stars of David ✡.

"The wom☐n should dress themselves m◇destly and decently in suitable cloth✡ng, not with their h☆ir braided, or with gold, pe☆rls, or ☐xpensive cloth☐s, but with g◆◆d works, as is proper for w◆men who profess reverence for G◆d" (1 Timothy 2:9, 10, NRSV).

We are also different in what we choose to read, listen to, or watch. **What six things should we look for when choosing what we spend our time with?**

"Finally, brethren, whatever things are _____ , whatever things are _____ , whatever things are _____ , whatever things are _____ , whatever things are _____ , whatever things are of _____ report, if there is any virtue and if there is anything praiseworthy—meditate on these things" (Philippians 4:8).

Making Jesus My Best Friend

We are different when we follow the example of Jesus in the way we live. This is how the Bible says it. **Fill in the missing words after you look up the text in your Bibles.**

"[He or she] who _____ [he or she] abides in Him [Jesus] ought . . . also to_____ just as He walked" (1 John 2:6).

When we are different in the way that God wants us to be, we are like something that smells good—it is a pleasant, enjoyable smell to God. This is how the Bible says it: "We are the sweet smell of Christ" (see 2 Corinthians 2:15).

Being different does not mean we are strange, but we are special. If your father is a king, you would behave as a son or daughter of the king, because you are special. Well, God is our Father, and He is the King of the universe, so we are children of the King, and that makes us special.

Closing Activity

Use the words from this lesson and the list below to complete the crossword puzzle (one is already done for you). This puzzle is done by counting letters. There is only one word with three letters and one more word with nine letters.

GOD   WATCH   CLOTHES

           HEART   SABBATH

READ   JESUS   SPECIAL

JUST   DRESS   JEWELRY

PURE

TRUE   HONEST   ~~GOOD WORKS~~

GOOD   PEARLS   BEAUTIFUL

GOLD   LISTEN

           LOVELY

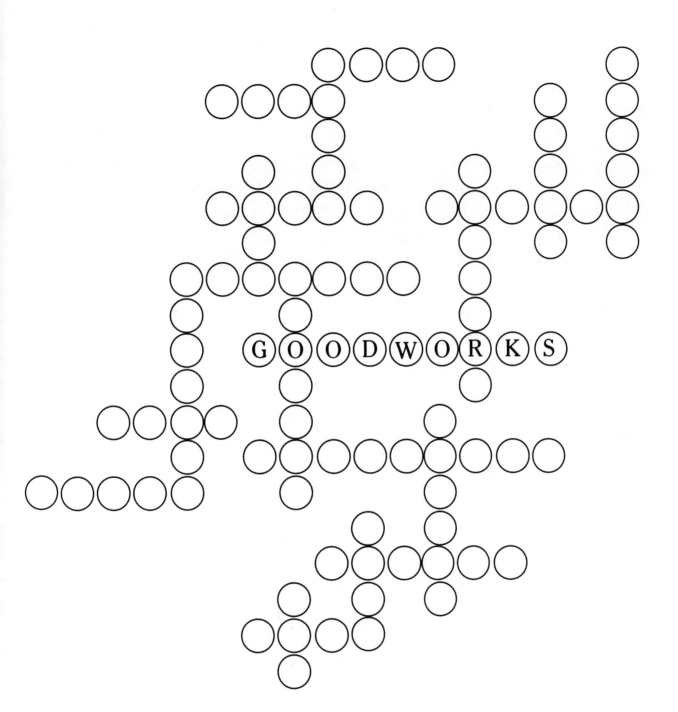

Don't forget to pray.

God's Special People

A New Beginning

Remember to Pray

Cleansing Water

That night for worship Mommy had a pitcher of sparkling water. "Mmmm," said Ashley, "that cold water looks good."

"It is what we are going to talk about tonight for worship," said Mommy. "I want us to make a list of all the things that water can be used to clean."

"I have one," said Daddy. "I used water today to wash my car. It cleaned off all the dirt and made it look pretty and shiny again."

"I have one too," said Ashley. When I got up this morning, I used water to take a shower and brush my teeth. I used water to clean me this morning."

"I used water to clean the dishes and the clothes," added Mommy.

"I have another one," remembered Daddy. "I also used water to give the dog a bath so that he would be nice and clean."

"And I also used water to help Mommy clean the floors," said Ashley.

"Just take a look at our list," said Mommy. "Look at all the things that in just one day water helped us to clean."

"Did you know that we can be clean on the inside, too?" asked Daddy. "When we accept Jesus and ask Him to forgive us, it is just like being washed clean. God cleans us and lets us start over."

Daddy opened the Bible and read, "'Be baptized, and wash away your sins'" (Acts 22:16). "You see," said Daddy, "being baptized makes us a sparkling clean Christian. Baptism is our way to say that we have made Jesus our very Best Friend, and it is God's way to clean up our sins."

"I want to tell everyone how much I love Jesus, and I also want Jesus to make me clean on the inside," said Ashley.

Think and Do

A New Chance

Have you ever wished you could do something again because you made a mistake the first time? Have you ever gotten the chance to fix a mistake, but then tried and found you couldn't fix it?

That's the way it is when we sin. Sometimes we can change things and make them better; sometimes we can't fix things at all. And often the results of what we have done remain, no matter what we do to fix things.

In the second lesson we learned that sin is missing the mark. And every time we miss the mark we leave a scar in our life. God wants to give us a chance to make our lives as if we had never sinned—no scars at all.

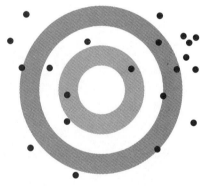

This is what happens when we are baptized:

Fill in the missing words after you look up the text.

"Be baptized, and _____ away your

_____" (Acts 22:16).

When we are baptized, it is as if we are given a brand-new target without any scars in it. We can also think of it as being born again—with no sin at all. That's why it is so important that we do this, because it is a new beginning for us.

The Preparation

How do we prepare for baptism? Well, these lessons are the first step. The next step is found in Mark 16:16.

Fill in the missing words where indicated by a blank line.

"[He or she] who believes _____ is baptized will _____ saved."

In order to be baptized, you must believe that God loves you, and you must want to love Him back.

The next step is found in Acts 2:38:

"_____ , and let every one of _____ be baptized in the name of Jesus Christ for the remission [forgiveness] of _____."

To repent means to understand and accept that what we did was wrong. Then we make the decision not to do it again, and ask God to help us with that decision.

Following Jesus' Example

Jesus was baptized even though He never missed the mark, in order to give us an example of what we should do. How was Jesus baptized?

"When He had been baptized, Jesus came up immediately from the water" (Matthew 3:16).

The fact that Jesus came up from the water teaches us that He went under the water to be baptized. The Bible teaches that baptism means a total going under water—that's how Jesus was baptized.

When the pastor baptizes you, he or she will do it in the name of God. He or she will say, "I baptize you 'in the name of the _____ and of the _____ and of the _____ _____' [Matthew 28:19]."

Join the Family

Another wonderful thing happens when you are baptized—you become part of God's family, His church.

"And the Lord added to the _____ daily those who were being _____ [baptized]" (Acts 2:47).

Your Decision

So now you can take this important step. You have completed these lessons that prepare you for baptism. You have come to believe that God loves you. You want to ask Him to help you so you won't sin again.

Read the baptismal vows, and if you understand and believe what each one says, put a check mark by it. If you are not sure you understand, ask your mom or dad for more explanation, and then put a check mark by each.

When you have checked all of them, have your mom or dad talk to your pastor to arrange a time you can be baptized.

Don't forget to pray.

Baptismal Vows

Please check all the ones that you believe and understand.

☐ 1. I believe in God, who is my loving Father; in His Son, Jesus Christ, who is my Best Friend; and in the Holy Spirit, who is my sweet Helper.

☐ 2. I believe that Jesus loved me so much that He died on the cross for my sins—those times that I miss the target.

☐ 3. I believe that Jesus forgave my sins and gave me a new heart when I opened the door and invited Him in.

☐ 4. I believe that Jesus will help me to live a good life so that others can see Him in me.

☐ 5. I believe that the Bible is God's love letter and a road map to show me where to go, and I will spend time in prayer and in reading it.

☐ 6. I believe that God gave the Ten Commandments to me and that I am happiest when I obey them. I also believe that the Sabbath is my special day to spend with my forever Friend, Jesus.

☐ 7. I believe that death is like a sleep and that one

day soon Jesus will come to awaken all those that rest in Him.

☐ 8. I believe that Jesus will come soon to take me to live with Him forever, and I will tell others about Him so that they can also live with Jesus forever.

☐ 9. I believe that Jesus makes each of us special by giving us gifts that we can use for Him. One of those gifts is the gift of prophecy.

☐ 10. I believe that God wants me to love and support my church in all that I do.

☐ 11. I believe that Jesus wants me to take care of my body, so I will be careful to keep it healthy.

☐ 12. I believe in the basic beliefs as the Seventh-day Adventist Church teaches us, and I want to live by them.

☐ 13. I believe that Jesus gave me an example to follow when He was baptized, so I want to be like Him and follow that example.

☐ 14. I believe the Seventh-day Adventist Church has a special message to give to the world, and I want to become a member of the Seventh-day Adventist church that my family and I attend.

About the Authors

Claudio Consuegra has been a pastor, hospice and law-enforcement chaplain, and marriage and family counselor for 20 years. He holds a Bachelor of Arts in theology from Columbia Union College, Takoma Park, Maryland, and a Master of Science in counseling psychology with emphasis in marriage and family counseling from Radford University, Radford, Virginia; and is pursuing a Doctor of Ministry degree from Andrews University, Berrien Springs, Michigan. Currently Claudio pastors the Pathways church of Maple Grove in Minnesota; he is also the family ministries director for the Minnesota Conference of Seventh-day Adventists.

Pamela K. Consuegra, an educator with more than 20 years of experience as a teacher and administrator, has also written a series of books published by Concerned Communications. She holds a Bachelor of Arts in elementary education from Columbia Union College, and a Master of Science in education with emphasis in curriculum development from Radford University. Pamela is currently the superintendent of education for the Minnesota Conference of Seventh-day Adventists.

Claudio and Pamela have been married 22 years and have two daughters: Diana, a senior English education major at Columbia Union College (graduating May 2005); and Hadassah, a junior at Minnetonka Christian Academy, Minnetonka, Minnesota.

Answer Key

Page 11. spoke

Page 12. Bible; teach; wrong; helps; way; good

Page 13. things; down; me

Page 14. Across: 1. God. 2. Bible. 5. vision. 7. help. 10. Holy Spirit. 11. map.
Down: 1. guide. 3. love. 4. Prophet. 6. Jesus. 8. books. 9. dreams.

Page 15.

Page 18. All; wages

Page 19. sin; gift; life

Page 20. life; Son; believe; gave; Him; life

Page 21. He; cleanse; all; I; opens

Page 22.

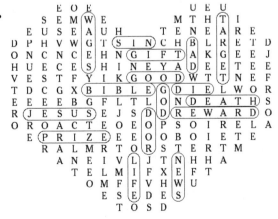

Page 25. heart; house; you; again; you

Page 26. Watch; pray; eye; all; angels

Page 27. Lord; heaven; archangel; God; dead; first; rise; meet; Lord

Page 28. alive; them; clouds; Lord; air; forever

Pages 30-32. "Looking for the blessed hope and glorious appearing of our great God and Savior Jesus Christ."
"He who testifies to these things says, 'Surely I am coming quickly.' Amen. Even so, come, Lord Jesus!"

Page 35. God; rested; blessed; seventh; sanctified

Pages 36, 37. day; work; your; breaking; please; delight; holy; own; idle; joy; custom

Page 38.

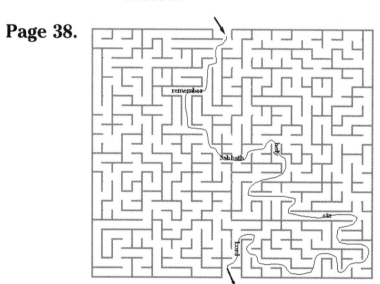

Page 39. Remember; Sabbath; holy; six; Lord

Page 43. Sabbath

Page 44. tithe

Page 45.

Page 46. eat; drink; do; God; body; home; you; lives

Page 47. herb; seed; tree; fruit; food

Page 48. Clean land animals must have hoofs that are divided and must chew their cud. Clean sea animals must have fins and scales. Some animals that are unclean are the camel, pig, rabbit, mole, mouse, snake, alligator, lizard, chameleon, tortoise, bat, weasel, ferret, eagle, seagull, vulture, buzzard, raven, owl, hawk, swan, pelican, stork, heron, crab, lobster, crayfish, shrimp, and snail.

Page 49.

Page 52. God; life; being

Page 53. dust; God; sleeps; dead

Page 54. dead; we

Page 55.

```
        E E H N C I B W
        R A R B E I N G
        T T W H I N K N
        F A M I L Y N Y
        T S C A R Y R I
D R G N E A A E T E F C O B A E T M
E E R D C C C S B N E R N R E E G I
A U O S L E E P E I H E D E A T H E
D N U D A A O A G A O A U A I A N N
Q I N X Y H E Y I E S T U T P R F D
O O D E D U S T N U E I U H C D D S
D N G O D M V A S R L O S J E S U S
O E E I N A G Z T R I N S P T N S O
        N A H H S F A C
        E E I C A E T A
        N F O R E V E R
        F H E A V E N E
        P A N Y E C T F
```

Page 59. right; true

Page 60. come; the Son, Jesus; Satan

Page 61. Jesus; the law of liberty, or the Ten Commandments; come; time

Page 62.

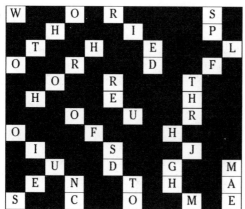

Page 63.

W O R S H I P   T H E
L O R D ,   F O R   T H E
H O U R   O F   H I S
J U D G M E N T   H A S
C O M E .

Page 66. gifts; your; ask

Page 67.

Page 68. wisdom; knowledge; faith; healing; working miracles; prophecy; discerning spirits; tongues; interpreting tongues; evangelism; ministry; teaching; apostleship; dreams; visions

Page 71.

Page 74. you; own

Pages 75, 76. beauty; hair; hearts; gentle; deep; women; modestly; clothing; hair; pearls; expensive; clothes; good; God; true; noble; just; pure; lovely; good

Page 77. says; walk

Page 79.

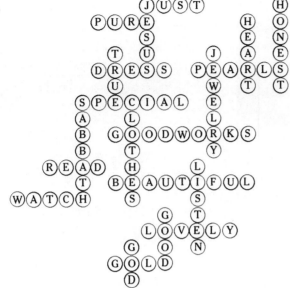

Page 82. wash; sins

Page 83. and; be; Repent; you; sins

Page 84. Father; Son; Holy; Spirit

Page 85. church; saved